NATIVE AMERICAN CODE TALKERS

NATIVE AMERICAN CODE TALKERS

ESSENTIAL LIBRARY OF
★ ★ WORLD
WAR II ★ ★

Essential Library

An Imprint of Abdo Publishing
abdopublishing.com

BY M. M. EBOCH

CONTENT CONSULTANT

THOMAS A. BRITTEN
ASSOCIATE PROFESSOR OF HISTORY AND
DEPARTMENT CHAIR
UT BROWNSVILLE

abdopublishing.com

Published by Abdo Publishing, a division of ABDO, PO Box 398166, Minneapolis, Minnesota 55439. Copyright © 2016 by Abdo Consulting Group, Inc. International copyrights reserved in all countries. No part of this book may be reproduced in any form without written permission from the publisher. Essential Library™ is a trademark and logo of Abdo Publishing.

Printed in the United States of America, North Mankato, Minnesota

052015
092015

THIS BOOK CONTAINS
RECYCLED MATERIALS

Cover Photo: US Marine Corps
Interior Photos: US Marine Corps, 1, 3; US Coast Guard/AP Images, 6; Red Line Editorial 8, 35; US Marine Corps History Division, 13, 33, 38, 42; North Wind Picture Archives, 16; M & Y News Ltd/Rex Features/AP Images, 21; Dr. David Hamer/National Museum of the US Air Force, 22; Corbis, 23; US Navy/AP Images, 25, 98 (right); Western History Collection/The Denver Public Library (X-32967), 26, (Z-15644), 29; J. N. Choate/Corbis, 31; Clyde Mueller/The Santa Fe New Mexican/AP Images, 45; Cpl. Robert M. Howard/US Marine Corps History Division, 46; nm319g000s003b001f0011i0001, Northern Arizona University, Cline Library, 52; Saunders/US Marine Corps History Division, 55; Salvatore Gatto/US Marine Corps History Division, 57; Philip Johnston Collection, Northern Arizona University, Cline Library, 58, 60; Sgt. Williams/US Marine Corps History Division, 64; PFC Lawrence M. Ashman/US Marine Corps History Division, 67, 72, 99 (top); Zerbe/US Marine Corps History Division, 68; Dreyfuss/US Marine Corps History Division, 75; Cecil Calvert Beall/Library of Congress, 77; US Army, 78; US Army Signal Corps, 83, 98 (left); William Meadows/US Army, 85; United States Marine Corps History Division, 87; Greg Ward/DK Images, 92; Manuel Balce Ceneta/AP Images, 93; PhotoQuest/Getty Images, 94; Lev Radin/Shutterstock Images, 97, 99 (bottom)

Editor: Kari A. Cornell
Series Designers: Kelsey Oseid and Maggie Villaume

Library of Congress Control Number: 2015931119

Cataloging-in-Publication Data

Eboch, M. M.
 Native American code talkers / M. M. Eboch.
  p. cm. -- (Essential library of World War II)
Includes bibliographical references and index.
ISBN 978-1-62403-794-8
1. World War, 1939-1945--Participation, Indian--Juvenile literature. 2. United States--Armed Forces--Indians--Juvenile literature.
3. World War, 1939-1945--Cryptography--Juvenile literature. 4. Indian code talkers--Juvenile literature.
I. Title.
940.54--dc23

CONTENTS

US soldiers unload supplies during the invasion of Iwo Jima in February 1945. Code talkers played a vital role in the success of this mission.

IN THE HEAT OF BATTLE

The Navajo code talkers were far from home. Most of them had never left the Navajo Nation in the southwestern United States before joining the US Marines. At boot camp in California, they had learned they were to be part of a special, secret team. They used their native language, Navajo, to develop a code for transmitting messages. The US military hoped the enemy would not be able to decipher this unusual code.

Now, in February 1945, they were part of a force ready to attack Iwo Jima. On a map, Iwo Jima is a tiny speck of an island in the Pacific Ocean. Its total area is only about eight square miles (21 sq km). Yet it would be the site of one of the most important battles of World War II.

Japan controlled Iwo Jima at the beginning of 1945. The island is approximately 760 miles (1,220 km) south of Japan, making it an important strategic site for both the Axis and the Allied forces.

MONGOLIA

SOVIET
UNION

MANCHURIA

KOREA

JAPAN

CHINA

TOKYO

NAGASAKI

BONIN ISLANDS

OKINAWA

IWO JIMA

BURMA

THAILAND
FRENCH
INDOCHINA

PHILIPPINES

MARIANA ISLANDS

SAIPAN

GUAM

MALAYSIA

BRUNEI

BORNEO

NEW GUINEA

The tiny island of Iwo Jima became an important strategic base for Allied troops during

The Axis forces included Japan, Germany, and Italy, while the Allied forces included the United Kingdom, the United States, the Soviet Union, China, and France. World War II had begun in 1939 when Germany invaded Poland. Alliances formed quickly on both sides of the conflict, though the United States would not join the war until late in 1941.

The United States held the Mariana Islands, farther south. It used B-29 bomber planes to make raids on Japan from the Marianas. These long-distance planes could make the 3,000-mile (4,800 km) journey in 16 hours. However, the US planes had to pass near Iwo Jima. Japanese fighter planes, called Zeros, could take off from Iwo Jima to intercept the B-29s and attempt to shoot them down. Many of the crippled bombers crashed into the sea.

IWO JIMA, SULFUR ISLAND

Iwo Jima means "sulfur island." The name comes from the sulfur smell, similar to the odor of rotten eggs, which permeates the island. The battle for Iwo Jima began on February 19, 1945, and lasted more than a month. The battle, which the United States won, resulted in the deaths of approximately 21,000 Japanese troops and 6,800 US troops.[1] Iwo Jima was managed by the United States from 1945 until 1968, when it was returned to Japan. Japan officially changed the name of the island to its Japanese form, Iō-tō, in 2007. The island is still widely known as Iwo Jima. It is currently a Japanese military base and can be visited only with military permission. Many of the Japanese who died in the battle are still entombed in the catacombs on Iwo Jima.

If the United States could capture Iwo Jima, it would stop the attacks from Japanese Zeros. The United States could take over the island as a base. This would put medium-range bombers close enough to attack Japan. In addition, short-distance US fighter planes could accompany the heavy bombers flying to

Japan to protect them. Finally, holding Iwo Jima would help the United States blockade Japan by air and sea. The tiny island was a key to winning the war.

Since Iwo Jima was equally as important to Japan's success, the island was heavily guarded. Taking control of the tiny chunk of land would not be easy. Lieutenant General Holland Smith, commander of the US landing forces, said, "This will be the bloodiest fight in Marine Corps history. We'll catch seven kinds of hell on the beaches, and that will be just the beginning. The fighting will be fierce, and the casualties will be awful, but my Marines will take the damned island!"[2]

GIANT BOMBERS

The Boeing B-29 Superfortress airplane was an important tool in World War II. Most B-29s carried ten machine guns, a cannon, and up to 20,000 pounds (9,000 kg) of bombs. They had a flying range of 3,700 miles (6,000 km). This allowed the planes to make long-distance raids on Japan from bases in China or islands in the Pacific Ocean.

A B-29 called *Enola Gay* dropped an atomic bomb on Hiroshima, Japan, on August 6, 1945. A B-29 called *Bockscar* dropped another atomic bomb on Nagasaki, Japan, three days later. Those devastating bombings ended the war. The *Enola Gay* is now on display at the National Air and Space Museum (NASM) of the Smithsonian Institution in Washington, DC. *Bockscar* is on display at the National Museum of the US Air Force in Ohio.

CODE TALKERS ON DECK

The Navajo code talkers were the United States' secret weapon. To make sure Japanese forces did not figure out their battle plans, US forces communicated using code. The code talkers translated messages for the commanders as US forces conducted air raids lasting ten weeks. Then battleships attacked the island. They fired more than 22,000 rounds of shells and dropped more than 6,900 short tons (6,300 metric tons) of bombs before soldiers ever set foot on the island. The US

NAVAJO CEREMONIES

Traditional Navajo people conduct ceremonies throughout the year, some lasting many days. Songs and prayers often accompany day-to-day acts, such as building a home and planting crops.

The Navajo do not perform ceremonies when burying the dead, however. They believe the spirit of a person lingers after death. These spirits are dangerous to anyone who comes near the body. Because of this belief, the dead are buried in unmarked graves by people other than close family.

In wartime, soldiers have constant contact with dead bodies. Combat troops are often surrounded by bodies—those of their own side and of the enemy. They might have to spend days in a foxhole next to the body of a friend who had been killed. Landing on an island might require wading through floating bodies and crossing beaches littered with the dead.

Many Navajo soldiers found comfort in traditional rituals. They brought along pouches of sacred corn pollen and held ceremonies during their tours of duty.

forces hoped to weaken the Japanese defense with this advanced action, but only a land battle among soldiers would determine which side controlled the island. In preparation, 450 ships gathered with 70,000 US Marines ready to land.

As the convoy surrounded Iwo Jima, some code talkers made their way to the ships' decks at 4:30 a.m. They performed an ancient ritual greeting to Father Sun, one of their gods. The Navajo soldiers placed dabs of sacred corn pollen on their tongues and the tops of their heads and made an offering to the east. This ritual was designed to give them clear speech, clear thought, and a safe path to walk.

Soon after, code talkers Thomas Begay and Johnny Manuelito were at their post on the top deck of the ship. Begay later said,

> I couldn't believe how ugly and forbidding that place looked. It made me very uncomfortable, and then something happened that confirmed that feeling. Johnny and I had our radio net operating when a shell, fired from the island, bounced off just below where we were standing. It bounced off the next deck below and exploded on the third bounce. We would have been the first casualties of Iwo Jima if that shell had exploded on impact. Things like that made you glad you performed your ceremony.[3]

The first wave of US Marines hit the beaches at approximately 9:00 a.m. on February 19, 1945. The island itself looked bleak. Due to past volcanic activity, the beaches were black sand. The air was hot and humid, day and night, and the island reeked of rotten eggs from the sulfur released by active volcanic vents.

The danger, however, came from the thousands of Japanese soldiers entrenched on the island. In the months leading up to the attack, they had built a network of tunnels, which joined underground concrete shelters. Antitank mines were buried in the sandy slopes. Every jumble of rock and brush held peepholes and gunports. The Japanese had 800 positions from which to fire weapons. Crossing any open space meant exposing oneself to gunfire. This tiny island was one of the strongest Japanese defenses.

The struggle began when the US soldiers reached the beach. They had trouble gaining traction in the volcanic ash soil. An earthen terrace approximately 15 feet (5 m)high blocked their way. Vehicles bogged down on the beach. Soldiers had to wade through the deep sand and up steep slopes, carrying more

Corporal Henry Blake Jr. of Fort Defiance, Arizona, and Private First Class (PFC) George H. Kirk of Leuppe, Arizona, send messages in code in the Pacific Theater in December 1943.

than 100 pounds (45 kg) of gear. At least they faced little resistance from the Japanese—at first.

UNDER FIRE

Then the Japanese attacked. They had let the Marines reach the beach in order to spring a trap on them. Marines caught on the beach had little shelter besides their stranded vehicles and the bodies of their fallen comrades. Still, the Marines held the beachhead. They had managed to land 30,000 soldiers and a mountain of supplies.[4]

All those troops needed to communicate with each other and with commanders on the ships who could assist them by firing their huge guns on enemy positions. But they could not let the Japanese understand their messages. They needed radio operators who could quickly translate messages into and out of code. They needed the Navajo code talkers.

The US ships sent waves of bombers over the island to hold back the Japanese. Some of these planes failed to pull up in time and crashed into a mountain. Between bombings, more US troops tried to land. Six waves of Marines would attempt to land on the island every five minutes. The second wave included the first of the code talkers.

NUMBER UNKNOWN

It is hard to say for certain how many Navajos worked as code talkers in World War II. Different recruiters had their own records. Navajos who enlisted before May 1942 might have been tapped for the code-talking program later. It is even more difficult to guess how many Navajos served altogether, in every branch of the military. In many districts, Navajos were listed on Selective Service records as white.

Some landing craft never reached shore. Code talker Merril L. Sandoval was in a landing craft that overturned after being hit by enemy gunfire. He made it to the beach, but lost his radio equipment. Those code talkers who did arrive with their radios had to carry everything across the ashy sand while under fire. They set up in two-man teams. Soon the code talkers were reporting information to their counterparts in other areas. This system of linked code talkers was known as the Navajo Net.

The messages flew furiously:

Receiving mortar fire.

We have lost four radiomen and one telephone man. Unable to estimate equipment damage as yet.

Need bulldozer on Green Beach immediately.

Receiving steady machine gun and rifle fire from 132B[5]

The code talkers were not fighting, but that did not mean they were safe. Shells and bombs exploded overhead. Tanks smashed into the Japanese entrenchments. Marines threw grenades, wielded flamethrowers, and planted explosives. They made progress yard by yard, with little shelter. The code talkers worked among the chaos. If they could not keep the radios up and working and send accurate, unbreakable codes, the battle could be lost. They were a long way from home and in a battle that could help determine the fate of the world.

SECRETS OF WAR

People have had the need to communicate quickly over long distances for centuries, especially in times of war. During battles, commanders may need to signal troops who cannot hear verbal commands over the noise of fighting. In ancient times, military leaders used fire, columns of smoke, or hand gestures to signal soldiers. During the American Revolutionary War, the number of lanterns hung in a church tower signaled whether the British were coming by land or sea. In the Civil War, a union officer developed a code that used flags during the day and torches at night. This was effective enough that the US Army established the Signal Corps branch.

Other means of communication have included mirrors, rockets, bugle calls, carrier pigeons, and messengers on foot or horseback. All of these methods had limitations. For one thing, messages could easily be seen or intercepted. Often the enemy could easily understand an intercepted message, if it was not in code or the code was easy to break. Finally, many of these methods were limited in distance and required a clear line of sight between the sender and receiver.

Sending codes in a language the enemy was unlikely to understand made the code more secure. In World War I, the American military stumbled on the idea of using Native American languages. In 1918, American forces needed to make a surprise attack on a German stronghold in France. The Germans had been able to intercept and decode most of the Allied messages.

Then one night, a captain overheard two Choctaw soldiers speaking their native language. When he found out the battalion had eight men who spoke Choctaw, he had an idea. The eight men were shifted to different areas where they could send and receive messages between the forces. The German code experts could not understand the language, and within 24 hours, the battle had turned in favor of the Allies.

US SIGNAL CORPS

The Army Signal Corps is still active today. The Signal Corps School at Fort Gordon trains soldiers in how to send and receive voice and data information. Soldiers may work on computer operations including information systems and worldwide networks. Training can include radio and television equipment use or repair. One field of study focuses on satellite communication systems. Others cover documentary photography and video.

Choctaw code talkers continued working for the remainder of the war. In all, 14 of them worked in communications. The code needed work, however, because the Choctaw language did not have words for military terms such as *artillery* and *machine gun*. The Choctaw were sent on a training mission to expand their code, but the war ended before they returned to the front lines. Some Comanche soldiers also used their language to send messages in Europe during World War I.

The Native American soldiers were told to keep their role in the war secret so the method could be used again. However, Germans identified the languages that had been used. In the next decades, many Germans visited America to study Native American languages. Though these visitors claimed to be tourists or scholars, they were really on assignment for their government. Germany hoped to prevent the use of Native American languages in the future.

By 1941, the Germans had studied most Native American languages. However, the Navajo language was still little known except among native speakers.

TECHNOLOGICAL ADVANCES

Code making and code breaking got more advanced with the use of machinery. Wireless radios allowed messages to be sent longer distances. However, radios also made it easier for the enemy to intercept those messages. In 1919, a US military report noted, "There was every reason to believe every decipherable message or word going over our wires also went to the enemy. Codes became even more important and increasingly complicated."[1]

CHOCTAW CODE TALKERS

The United States had an advantage during World War I. Hundreds of Native American tribes spoke languages that few people outside of those tribes understood. Some of these languages had never been written down. The use of Native American code talkers was barely explored in World War I, but officials recognized the possibilities. One officer reported on tests with the Choctaw: "It is believed had the regiment gone back into the line, fine results would have been obtained. We were confident the possibilities of the telephone had been obtained without its hazards."[2]

A German engineer developed the Enigma machine for coding messages. An operator typed a message into the machine and then scrambled the message using wheels with different letters. A receiver who knew the specific settings of those wheels could translate the coded message. The German military adopted the Enigma in the 1920s.

WIRELESS RADIOS

Early radios were large and heavy. They were also fragile, because they depended on glass tubes to control the electric current. They needed open ports for ventilation, so they were sensitive to moisture. One radio commonly used during World War II weighed 80 pounds (36 kg). It could be powered by batteries or by a hand-cranked generator. The generator, battery, accessory box, and 24-foot (7 m) collapsible antenna also had to be carried. This radio could transmit voice messages and Morse code for more than 100 miles (160 km).

Even these codes could sometimes be broken. A German spy provided stolen Enigma operating manuals. Eventually, the Polish Cipher Bureau was able to build a replica of the machine. With tensions rising in Europe, the Poles shared their secrets with the British government.

Using the replica to read German military messages required identifying the correct settings for each code. During World War II, the British government recruited many mathematicians to work on code breaking. Using early computers, they worked out all the possible settings for the Enigma. The Germans, believing their code was secure, used Enigma for many communications. In reality, the Allies were breaking these codes, providing them with many military advantages. Some experts claim the information learned by breaking the Enigma code shortened the war by approximately two years.

BRITAIN'S CODE BREAKERS

Understanding the Enigma machine was only the first step in breaking Germany's codes. There were 159 million possible settings for the wheels. The cipher for the messages changed at least once a day during the war. Thousands of people, both military and civilian volunteers, listened to German radio messages. They wrote down every letter and number. These codes then went to Bletchley Park, a mansion in the English countryside. There, mathematicians and other scholars worked on the code. To help break the code, they used an early form of a computer, which could run through all the possible configurations quickly. The most likely results were then hand-tested. To prevent the Germans from realizing their code had been broken, an imaginary spy network was created. Reports were shown as coming from the head spy, rather than the code breakers.

The code breakers at Bletchley Park, many of whom were women, became experts at deciphering German military messages using the Enigma.

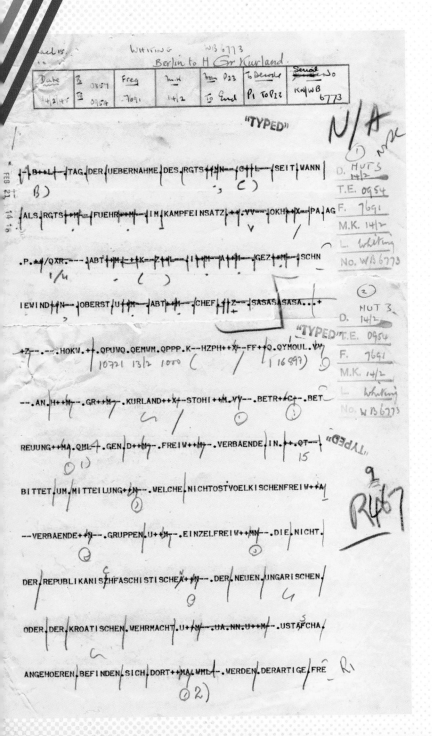

Japan also depended on codes for military successes. During World War II, the Japanese had a code that disguised messages as weather forecasts. For example, "East Wind – Rain" referred to relations between Japan and the United States.

Japan attacked the US naval base at Pearl Harbor, near Honolulu, Hawaii, on December 7, 1941. Because this attack was a complete surprise to the United States, it devastated the US naval base. Nearly 20 naval vessels and almost 200 airplanes were destroyed, and more than 2,000 American soldiers and sailors died.[3] This drew the United States into a war that had been raging in Europe for more than two years.

Japan failed to completely destroy the US fleet at Pearl Harbor. All of the US Pacific Fleet's aircraft carriers had been away from port. Oil storage depots,

This message was sent by German troops using the Enigma machine on February 14, 1945.

German soldiers use an Enigma machine on the battlefield during World War II. One man types while the other writes down the decoded or encoded message.

shipyards, and submarine docks also survived. But Japan kept up the pressure, taking over land in the South Pacific. Within a few days, Japan controlled Guam, Wake Island, Guadalcanal, Hong Kong, and the Philippines. All of these places had been under the control of the United States or the United Kingdom.

The Japanese Ministry of War planned a trap to draw out and finish off the remaining US fleet at Midway Island. However, US cryptographers broke the Japanese naval code. US intelligence intercepted and decoded radio transmissions warning of the new attack. With strong reinforcements, the United States was able to win the Battle of Midway, June 4 to June 7, 1942, and cripple the Japanese armada.

The battle for the South Pacific was far from over, however. The United States had broken the Japanese code, but the Japanese excelled at breaking US codes. If one side could create an unbreakable code, it would have a huge advantage in the rest of the war.

On December 7, 1941, Japan launched a surprise attack on Pearl Harbor. The USS *Arizona* was sunk in the attack.

Navajo men ride horses near Ship Rock, Arizona, in the early 1900s. Ship Rock is part of the Navajo reservation.

THE PEOPLE

People have lived in North America for at least thousands of years. By the time European settlers arrived, as many as 10 to 20 million Native Americans lived in what is now the United States. These people spoke at least 250 different languages. Some languages were related, but others were vastly different. Many of these languages have disappeared, but dozens are still used.

When Europeans arrived in North America, fights broke out between the Native American people and the newcomers. Natives were killed or pushed off their land. Some were forced onto areas of land called reservations. Many also died from European diseases. Today there are fewer than 2 million Native Americans. Only eight native languages within the area of the continental United States have more than 9,000 native speakers. Of these, only Navajo has more than 25,000 native speakers.[1] None had a written form before the arrival of Europeans.

By the late 1800s, the US government had forced most native tribes onto reservations. Native children were often brought to government- or church-supported boarding schools. These schools attempted to replace traditional native culture with mainstream American culture. As a result, students were not allowed to speak their native languages. They had to cut their hair and wear uniforms instead of their traditional clothing. They were called by English names and had to follow Christian religious practices. Some teachers humiliated students and ridiculed their traditions. The students might not see their families for up to four years. Richard Henry Pratt, founder of the Carlisle Indian Industrial School, is quoted as saying, "I believe in immersing the Indian in our civilization and when we get them under, holding them there until they are thoroughly soaked."[2] Some of these boarding schools continued until the 1930s.

Some native families sent their children to school willingly. They recognized that learning English could be valuable, especially if the children ever wanted or needed to leave the reservations. At school,

LANGUAGE FAMILIES

Language families are groups of languages that are related. An example would be the Romance languages, which include Spanish, French, and Italian. All are descended from Latin. Even the languages within one family can vary greatly. For example, English, which is a Germanic language, is part of a family of languages called the Indo-European family. The very different languages of Dutch and Hindi are also part of the Indo-European family. Scholars believe nine major language families existed in what is now the United States when Europeans first arrived. The Navajo language comes from the Athabaskan family, the same as that of the various Apache peoples. There were also smaller families, and a few languages that were unrelated to any other.

A Navajo family is pictured in front of their home on the Navajo reservation in the southwestern United States during the 1940s.

the students would learn to read and write and obtain training in farming, carpentry, or other job skills.

PHILIP JOHNSTON'S BIG IDEA

Philip Johnston grew up on the Navajo reservation as the son of a missionary. He was one of the few non-Navajos who spoke their language well, though he was not fluent. Johnston served with the US Army in World War I. Later, he often visited the Navajo reservation. He gave lectures around the Southwest, describing his experiences among the Navajo and showing photographs. He had heard about the army's use of the Comanche code talkers. After the attack on Pearl Harbor, Johnston contacted the Marine Corps about using Native American languages for communications. He prepared a proposal discussing native languages in general but focusing on Navajo in particular.

Navajo had the advantage of a large group of native speakers, which would make it easier to recruit enough code talkers. Even better, Navajo is an especially hard language to learn. It is complex, with tonal qualities. Tones can be high, low, rising, or falling, and the pitch can change the meaning of words. The words for *medicine* and *mouth* are pronounced in the same way, except with a different tone. Some words use a glottal stop, a small catch of the breath. Words that sound identical to a non-Navajo can have completely different meanings if they include a glottal stop. A written version of the language requires accent marks and phonetic symbols.

WHO ARE THE PEOPLE?

Linguists are not certain about the origin of the word *Navajo*, also sometimes spelled "Navaho." Some believe it to be Spanish. Others suggest it came from another native group, the Tewa. The term may refer to farmed fields. One thing is certain; the name did not come from the people now known as Navajo. They use different names for themselves, including Naabeeho´ Dine'é or Diné. Diné Bizaad is their term for their native language. *Diné* means "The People" or "Children of the Holy People."

The US government required Native American children to attend government-run
boarding schools such as the Yankton Sioux Agency in South Dakota.

Even the vocabulary is complex. Different verbs are used to describe picking up a handful of soft mud versus picking up a stick. A different verb form is used depending on whether one, two, or more than two people are performing an action. This complexity meant few outsiders could speak the language fluently. Nor would it be easy to learn Navajo quickly. At best, outsiders spoke "trade Navajo," which allowed them to buy and sell goods and hold simple conversations. Chester Nez, a Navajo man who served as a code talker, explained, "When a Navajo asks whether you speak his language, he uses these words: 'Do you hear Navajo?' Words must be heard before they can be spoken. Many of the sounds in Navajo are impossible for the unpracticed ear to distinguish."[3]

After World War I, the Germans and Japanese sent many students to the United States to learn native languages. Those languages, consequently, were no longer secure for military use. Yet Navajo was still believed to be too complex and unknown, providing the needed security. At the beginning of World War II, perhaps 30 non-Navajos spoke the language fluently, and none of them were Japanese.

Johnston was asked to provide a demonstration of his proposed system. He recruited Navajo volunteers. They were given an hour to prepare several field messages for transmission. However, the messages contained words that had no Navajo equivalent. For example, one message was, "Tanks artillery weapon carrying vehicles with ammunition will be landed in next wave."[4]

The volunteers asked for more time to work out the necessary language. When they were ready, two Navajo were taken into another room. They received the messages in English and used a field telephone to transmit them.

The receiving Navajo wrote down the messages in English. They were not word-for-word correct, but they were very close. This convinced the Marine Corps officials the idea was worth pursuing. The military officials decided to start by enlisting 30 Navajos, who would receive training and develop the code.

But would the Navajo want to participate? Native Americans as a whole had only gained the right to legal citizenship in 1924, though some tribes and individuals gained citizenship earlier. Some states still did not let them vote. Some tribes argued they were sovereign nations and the United States government had no right to force Native Americans to serve. And, according to some tribal treaties, tribal members were not allowed to use guns either for or against the US government.

Technical Sergeant Philip Johnston was instrumental in beginning the Navajo code talkers program.

NAVAJO NATION
A SACRED HOME

CURRENT POPULATION
More than 250,000 tribal members.[5]

SIZE
The largest reservation in the United States, covering more than 27,000 square miles (70,000 sq km).

LOCATION
The area where Utah, New Mexico, and Arizona meet. This region includes four mountains sacred to the Navajo.

GOVERNMENT
The Navajo tribal government operates under a constitution. There is a president, vice president, and council of 88 delegates. This government runs a court system, police force, and college.

UTAH

COLORADO

ARIZONA

NEW MEXICO

NAVAJO NATION

A RESOLUTION TO DEFEND

In 1940, the Navajo Tribal Council passed a resolution swearing to defend the United States. In part, it read as follows:

Whereas, it has become common practice to attempt national destruction through the sowing of seeds of treachery among minority groups, such as ours, and

Whereas, we hereby serve notice that any un-American movement among our people will be resented and dealt with severely, and

Now, Therefore be it resolved that the Navajo Indians stand ready as they did in 1918 to aid and defend our government and its institutions against all subversive and armed conflict and pledge our loyalty to the system which recognizes minority rights and a way of life that has placed us among the greatest people of our race.[6]

Yet many Native Americans signed up to be soldiers. Many tribes had strong warrior traditions. Warriors were respected as the protectors of their people. Boys were trained to have the physical, mental, and spiritual strength needed to be warriors. Job opportunities were sparse on reservations. Some Native American men enlisted to earn money and improve living conditions for their families. Native Americans volunteered for the military because they wanted to defend their communities and their traditional homelands. Many also felt patriotism toward the United States, despite the racism they faced and the long history of conflict between Native American and non-native peoples.

Some Navajo even saw joining the military as a way to honor their ancestors and restore tribal pride. Samuel Holiday, who was in a later group of code talkers, said,

Sometimes I think of how strong and resilient my ancestors were to have traveled many miles for days at a time during the Long Walk, suffering from hunger, brutality, and poor living conditions. Many died, but others came home. I wanted to somehow pay them back for their sacrifice and fight with the modern weapons I was now given but this time win against the enemy.[7]

Others felt they were defending their own people. John Brown Jr. later said, "I like to think about among Indian Native people, that I defended their religion, their belief, their land, their stories and all that."[8]

THE LONG WALK

The Navajo had many clashes with white settlers in the mid-1800s. These led to the Navajo War in 1860. The Navajo battled against the US cavalry for the last time in 1864. The Navajo holed up in Canyon de Chelly, a secure stronghold with only one entrance. The cavalry, led by US Army colonel Kit Carson, destroyed crops, killed livestock, and burned Navajo homes. Without food or shelter, the trapped Navajo finally surrendered. They were forced to leave their homeland. They walked 300 miles (480 km) to a camp where other tribes were being held. Many Navajo died on the journey or at the camp. Approximately 8,500 Navajo started out on this trip, which became known as the Long Walk.[9] Four years later, they signed a treaty establishing the Navajo Reservation. They were allowed to return to a reduced area of their homeland. Only 6,000 people survived to make the long trip home.[10]

382nd PLATOON U.S.M.C. SAN DIEGO
1942
U.S MARINES — FIRST TO FIGHT

ng in San Diego,

RECRUITMENT AND TRAINING

The recruiter for the Marine Corps arrived at Fort Defiance, Arizona, in April 1942. First Sergeant Frank Shinn had not been told the specific reason for recruiting 30 Navajo. He knew, however, that they had to be fluent in both English and Navajo. He guessed a special program was being designed for them.

Soldiers enlisting for the first time had to be between the ages of 17 and 32. Some Navajo men lied about their age in order to make the cut. Most of them had no birth certificates, making it easier to get away with the ruse. The youngest got in at age 15.

Carl Gorman pretended to be younger than his true age of 35. From the recruiter's talk of "special duty," he thought they might end up with desk jobs in Washington, DC. But any job was appealing, since he was unemployed. The recruiter talked about travel, meeting interesting people, and learning new skills. But, Gorman said, "What did it for me was the dress uniform on the poster. Crisp white hat and gloves, brass buttons against the deep blue material, boy he looked sharp! I wanted a uniform just like that."[1]

After two weeks, Shinn had recruited 29 Navajos. On May 4, 1942, these recruits traveled by bus to the Marine Recruit Depot near San Diego, California. Few had left the reservation before; now they were traveling hundreds of miles from home.

GETTING IN

Some Navajo were determined to join the military, even if they did not meet the standard requirements. The minimum weight requirement was 122 pounds (55 kg). Navajo tend to be smaller. Some gorged on food or water before the weigh in to try to meet the minimum. At 16, William Dean Wilson could have enlisted with his parents' permission, but they refused to sign the consent form. He managed to remove the note on his file stating that his parents had withheld consent.

A NEW LIFE

Their new life was challenging for some of the recruits. Eugene Crawford commented, "After the free life of the reservation, this place looked like a prison with all the guards, gates, and barbed wire fences."[2] At least they were together. Crawford had already served in the Reserve Officers' Training Corps (ROTC). He was able to give advice and comfort to those who were confused and lonely.

Experience at Native American boarding schools came in handy for those entering the military. Merril Sandoval explained that the military-style life at school prepared them for the Marines. "[School] was still kind of military basis. So when we were in the service everything just came natural, physically and morally and everything."[3] John Benally also noted, "We knew how to drill, not in true military fashion, but we knew how to drill."[4]

Traditional life on the reservation also helped prepare them for the military. Most Navajo were very fit. They might have to walk 30 miles (50 km) to get supplies from a trading post, so marching with full packs was not a new challenge. They were used to hunting and protecting livestock. When the first group of code talkers graduated on June 27, they had the best rifle range record of any outfit at the time.

Chester Nez remembered days of training that began at 5:30 a.m. and went until 7:30 p.m., with a half-hour lunch break. They ran along the beach carrying pails of sand and salt water. They practiced marching drills and went through an obstacle course. They learned to swim and then practiced abandoning ship by jumping into water from 30 feet (9 m) up. They did laundry with a scrub brush. They practiced target shooting with rifles and pistols and learned to throw hand grenades. They practiced hand-to-hand combat with bayonets. In survival training, they marched for miles across the desert with limited food and water, staying in improvised shelters. "It was like herding sheep all over again," Nez remembered.[5]

The Navajo soldiers also studied in the classroom. They learned Morse code and semaphore flag signals. They studied the various weapons and practiced disassembling and reassembling their rifles blindfolded. They learned to fix radios, though they did not yet know how important that skill would be.

SUCCESS

The mental challenges were the hardest, as boot camp was a culture shock. In Navajo culture, looking someone directly in the eyes is considered rude. Elders seldom shout when giving instructions. But at boot camp, drill instructors barked orders and insisted the recruits maintain eye contact.

Despite the challenges, the Navajo Marines did very well. The Recruit Depot commanding officer commented on their loyalty, group spirit, and physical fitness. All 29 Navajos graduated from boot camp together; normally 5 to 10 percent of recruits would not make it through.[7]

THE 30TH MAN

The original group of code talkers was intended to be made up of 30 men. It is not known why only 29 Navajo made up the original group. Chester Nez thought one had dropped out because he was uncomfortable with the specific dialect of Navajo being used. However, a 1942 progress report referred to "One Navajo Indian, Private Jesse Kennepah." He was already in training when the other 29 arrived. Kennepah was "transferred to the Amphibious Corps and assigned special duty in connection with communications."[8] It is possible he was originally intended to be one of the 30 code talkers.

Some Navajo soldiers appreciated their time in the Marines. They were generally treated with respect. During free time, they visited bars wearing their uniforms. Without the uniforms, they would have gotten thrown out like other Native Americans. Harold Foster said, "Once I was accepted into the Corps, I was treated like a real human being. The Marines gave me a sense of self-respect that I knew I could use the rest of my life. . . . The Marines gave me confidence that I could do what was asked of me and succeed."[9]

The base commanding officer, Colonel James L. Underhill, addressed the all-Navajo 382nd Platoon at their graduation. He said, "This is the first truly All-American platoon to pass through this Recruit Depot. It is, in fact, the first All-American platoon to enter the United States Marine Corps." He called them "one of the outstanding platoons in the history of this Recruit Depot" and praised their discipline, health, and quick learning. He ended with, "When the time comes that you go into battle with the enemy, I know that you will fight like true Navajos, Americans, and Marines."[10]

THE BLESSING WAY

Navajo tradition requires a religious ceremony before sending warriors into battle. Many families had Blessing Way ceremonies for the young soldiers before they left home. The ceremony is said to ensure good luck, good health, success, and harmony to the one who is "sung over." Blessing Ways may be performed for people leaving for the military, pregnant women shortly before their baby is due, and others. The ceremony lasts for two days and nights and includes singing, prayers, and a ritual bath. The Blessing Way chant recounts the Navajo origin oral history. The ceremony is said to have been held by the holy people when they first created humans.

CHESTER NEZ

1921–2014

Chester Nez was born on the Navajo reservation in New Mexico. His mother died when he was three. At age nine, he left for a Bureau of Indian Affairs (BIA) boarding school. Marine recruiters came to his high school in the spring of 1942. Nez was recruited as part of the original code talker program. He was not seriously injured during the war, but he was threatened at gunpoint by a fellow American who mistook him for a Japanese soldier. He remained in the Marines through the Korean War. He later worked in maintenance at the Veterans Affairs (VA) hospital in Albuquerque, New Mexico.

Nez was one of the few code talkers to write his memoir. "With the release of the secrecy surrounding the Navajo code, I became a bit of a celebrity," he said. "That could be embarrassing. I know that I did my duty, nothing more."[11] He answered requests to speak about the experience. But nightmares he'd had after the war returned until a Holy Way ceremony helped him find peace again.

Chester Nez died in 2014 at age 93. He was the last of the original 29 Navajo code talkers.

Navajo code talkers with the First Marine Division work to solve a problem as part of their studies through the Amphibious Scout School.

CREATING THE CODE

After their graduation ceremony, the new Marine privates went directly to special training. Most new recruits got a ten-day furlough, but the new code was considered too urgent. It was late June 1942, almost seven months after the attack on Pearl Harbor. US forces were struggling with the Japanese in the Pacific. At Midway Island, the United States had intercepted and decoded Japanese messages and staged a successful ambush. This put the American and Japanese naval fleets on a more equal footing, but the United States desperately needed an advantage.

The Navajo Marines went to Camp Elliott in San Diego, where they had one day free to rest. They played cards or horseshoes or wrote letters to their families. Nez's family thought he was still at school, since he had not had an opportunity to visit home after enlisting. However, these letters were never delivered, as the Marine Corps wanted to protect the secrecy of the special assignment.

Work started after breakfast on a Monday morning. The Navajos gathered in a building with barred windows. The room reminded Crawford of boarding school, where he had to wash his mouth out with soap if he spoke Navajo.

An officer described how military codes were made and used. Then he explained their special assignment: to develop a code based on their native language. The team needed to develop an alphabet using Navajo words for English letters. Then they would choose Navajo words as substitutes for common military terms. These words should be short so they could be transmitted quickly. The materials they used in the classroom would be kept in a locked safe at night. All information had to be memorized.

WHERE ARE THEY?

For security reasons, the code talkers' letters home were intercepted and withheld. After several months, families started to worry. When an official from the reservation requested information, Johnston replied, noting that he could not say much about the program. However, he said, "We hope, and have every reason to believe, that the Navajos will play a major role in Marine Corps operations. When the war is over, their story may rank with the great sagas of the battlefield."[1]

IMPOSSIBLE?

At first they could hardly believe this complex assignment. The same government that had forbidden them to speak their native language in school now depended on it for national security.

The challenges were immense. Most of the Navajo Marines had not graduated from high school. Few had ever left the reservation before boot camp. Nez said, "How could we, twenty-eight of whom had never worked with the military, develop a code robust enough to be used in battle? One that could be responsible for sending life-or-death messages? The task loomed ahead like a black unmarked cavern."[2]

They were left on their own to develop the code. They all worked together, without a leader. Crawford had worked with codes in the reserves and shared that knowledge. Another recruit, Oscar Ilthma, remembered that his father had sent radio messages during World War I. Specific words were, and still are, used to help distinguish between letters of the alphabet. For example, a radio operator might clarify, "That's C as in Charlie."

Wilsie Bitsie's father had worked on developing a phonetic alphabet for the Navajo language. Bitsie suggested they start by focusing on the alphabet. He also recommended that they agree to a uniform pronunciation for every code word. This would help avoid confusion between code talkers using slightly different dialects.

UNDER LOCK

The men themselves were also subject to heightened security. They were locked in, with lunch delivered to their classroom. Wherever they went, even to the restroom, they had to go in pairs. They could not leave the building without permission. They could not discuss the assignment with anyone outside their team. Any failure in security could mean spending the rest of the war in military prison.

NAVAJO CODE

The original Navajo code talkers worked long hours to create a code that would be impossible to break. The code was so well thought out that even those who spoke Navajo could not decipher it. The Navajo soldiers assigned a Navajo word for each letter of the English alphabet. For military and war-specific terms, the code talkers used Navajo words for birds, fish, or other wildlife. Here is a translation of the Navajo alphabet and words used for military aircraft.

MILITARY AIRCRAFT		
Military Term	**Navajo Pronunciation**	**Navajo Meaning**
Airplanes	(No-tah-de-ne-ih)	Air Force
Dive Bomber	(Gini)	Chicken Hawk
Torpedo Plane	(Tas-chizzie)	Swallow
Observation Plane	(Ne-as-jah)	Owl
Fighter Plane	(Da-he-tih-hi)	Hummingbird
Bomber	(Jay-sho)	Buzzard
Patrol Plane	(Ga-gin)	Crow
Transport	(Ateah)	Eagle

NAVAJO ALPHABET

	Navajo Pronunciation	Navajo Meaning		Navajo Pronunciation	Navajo Meaning
A	(Wol-la-chee)	Ant	N	(Nesh-che)	Nut
B	(Shush)	Bear	O	(Ne-she-jah)	Owl
C	(Moasi)	Cat	P	(Bi-so-dih)	Pig
D	(Be)	Deer	Q	(Ca-yeilth)	Quiver
E	(Dzeh)	Elk	R	(Gah)	Rabbit
F	(Ma-e)	Fox	S	(Dibsh)	Sheep
G	(Klizzio)	Goat	T	(Than-zie)	Turkey
H	(Lin)	Horse	U	(No-da-ih)	Ute
I	(Tkin)	Ice	V	(A-keh-di-glini)	Victor
J	(Tkele-cho-gi)	Jackass	W	(Gloe-ih)	Weasel
K	(Klizzie-yazzie)	Kid	X	(Al-an-as-dzoh)	Cross
L	(Dibeh-yazzie)	Lamb	Y	(Teah-as-zih)	Yucca
M	(Na-as-teo-si)	Mouse	Z	(Besh-do-gliz)	Zinc

The team worked through the alphabet letter by letter. To make memorization easier, they chose simple, common English words to stand for each letter of the English alphabet. Translating these into Navajo added the necessary complexity. The Navajo words would be unfamiliar to nearly everyone outside the Navajo Nation. In addition, even if someone got a hold of the written list, they would not know the proper pronunciations.

On the first day, the men chose the words that would represent the alphabet letters. Nez remembered an officer unlocking the room at the end of the day. "He collected the working papers we'd generated that day and locked them in a safe. Hearing that safe slam shut, I was again impressed by the seriousness of our mission."[3]

This page from the *Navajo Code Talkers' Dictionary* includes the Navajo code translation for various types of ships.

BIRDS, FISH, AND STARS

They memorized the letters along with the associated English words and Navajo words. Next they had to come up with more than 200 words as substitutes for terms that did not exist in Navajo. It would be slow to spell out commonly used military terms every time. Instead, code words would be used.

This part of the assignment was much more complicated than the basic alphabet. Crawford later said, "There were days when I thought my head would burst. All the memorizing and frustration trying to find Navajo words that would fit things like 'echelon' and 'reconnaissance.' Sometimes we would spend three or four hours on just one word!"[4]

When the 29 Navajo recruits got stuck, they asked for help. Three additional Navajo who had become soldiers earlier were assigned to the program. Wilson Price and Ross Haskie had gone to college before entering the military. Haskie had been a teacher before he joined the Marines. Felix Yazzie also helped, and the three provided more educational and military experience.

With this extra help, the code talkers continued developing the code. They tried to choose words that would be descriptive, aided by pictures of the ships and planes they had to name. They used bird names for the various types of aircraft. Ships became fish and water mammals. Bombs were "eggs" and grenades were "potatoes." A flare was a "light streak" and a hospital was a "place of medicine." Officers were called by terms based on their insignia for each rank. "Two Stars" was a major general, "One Star" was a brigadier general, and "Silver Eagle" was a colonel. The name used to represent the United States of America translated to "our mother."

The code was complex, but highly accurate. They were not simply speaking Navajo, but rather translating messages letter by letter. This preserved the exact meaning. William McCabe explained, "The message comes out word for word on the other end, and including the semicolons, commas, periods, question marks, everything. We get all those."[5] Using Navajo to translate English letters also meant Navajos from outside the program would not be able to understand messages.

A CODE WITHIN A CODE

For complete security, the code could not be cracked by any Navajo speaker who was not in the group. Although they could understand the Navajo words, the message would not make sense. An example of a code sentence as an untrained Navajo would hear it:

Message: Request artillery and tank fire at 123B, Company E move 50 yards left flank of Company D.

Same Message Encoded by Navajos: Ask for many big guns and tortoise fire at 123 Bear tail drop Mexican ear mouse owl victor elk 50 yards left flank ocean fish Mexican deer.[6]

PRACTICE AND MORE PRACTICE

Memorizing the code did not give the Navajo Marines any trouble. Since they had not grown up with a written form of Navajo, they were used to memorizing songs, prayers, and other information. They practiced coding, sending, and decoding messages in the classroom. Soon they could quickly send long messages accurately.

They practiced constantly, quizzing each other. "We knew that the strength of the group made us all sharp," Nez wrote. "And in combat, the code would only be as strong as both men using it—the one on the sending end and the one on the receiving end." He added, "It had to

These Native American soldiers from New Mexico, who served with the veteran First Marine Division, were part of the code-talking team on the island of Peleliu.

be automatic, without a conscious thought process. We were to be living code machines."[7]

The Marine observers were amazed at how well the code worked, and how quickly. Decoding machines often took hours. The Navajos could translate a code in minutes. US intelligence tried to break the code and failed. Adjustments to the

AN ACCIDENTAL SCARE

One of their field exercises resulted in unforeseen consequences. Wilsie Bitsie recalled the military police taking him and two colleagues to headquarters under guard. Bitsie assumed he was in trouble but had no idea what he had done. At headquarters, they wheeled in a tape machine. "One of the officers finally spoke and said that they had received word from the Coast Guard that strange, and perhaps hostile, radio messages had been intercepted that morning and the entire California coast had been put on 'Red Alert,'" he remembered. "They asked me to listen to the tape and identify the source, if possible. I sat there and listened, and it was us talking!"[8]

code would be made throughout the war, but the Navajo Marines had succeeded in their basic mission: they had developed a simple but secure code.

Along with their work on the code, the Navajo soldiers received additional combat training. They also worked with field telephones and radios, learning both their mechanics and their operation. Their training ended in September 1942. They received promotions from private to private first class. The code talkers were assigned to units within the First and Second Marine Divisions and Raider Battalions. They would soon head to the Pacific battlefields, where they would test the code in combat situations.

PFC Edmond John, PFC Wilsie H. Bitsie, and PFC Eugene R. Crawford served with the

RECRUITING MORE CODE TALKERS

The initial Navajo code talkers were so successful the Marines requested 200 more Navajo recruits for the program. Navajos John Benally and Johnny Manuelito were promoted to corporal and assigned to recruit and instruct the next group. They traveled to the Navajo Nation to recruit. Frank Shannon and Frank Shinn, who were Marines but not Navajos, also worked on recruitment.

Finding enough Navajos willing and able to be code talkers was not easy. Navajo families were spread out across a 27,000-square-mile (70,000 sq km) reservation, an area similar in size to West Virginia.[1] It did not make sense to expect people to come to a recruiter in a central location. Potential recruits might not be able to get to that site. They might not even hear about the recruitment drive.

Navajo recruits stand at attention during training camp drills at Camp Elliott in California, 1940.

A better method was developed that involved teams of Marines traveling within the Navajo communities. Boarding schools were especially targeted as a good place to find educated young men. Technically, recruits were supposed to have nine years of education, though in reality, some had less. The recruiters also went to work sites, trading posts, and social gatherings.

Recruitment efforts were more successful when the recruiters were Navajos in uniform. The recruiters could not explain the program because of its secrecy. Yet historian Sally McClain writes, "Seeing one of their own dressed in that uniform, walking straight and proud, sent many a Navajo to enlist on the spot."[2]

Like the first group of code talkers, new recruits had to first go through boot camp. Samuel Holiday was drafted into the military while he was at a trade school. He did not enjoy his boot camp training. "We were no longer individuals in control of our lives but robots who did what the instructors told us," he said.[3]

Still, he passed all his tests on the first try, and he realized he was luckier than some new soldiers. His prior life of riding horses, chopping wood, hauling water, and playing sports had prepared him physically. He also thought prayers and meditation had prepared him mentally. And the military was easier than the Bureau of Indian Affairs school because he did not have to worry about bullies.

After completing boot camp, Holiday learned he would be trained as a code talker. The training was conducted by two of the men who had helped design the code. Secrecy was still paramount. "Our classroom was in an isolated area with heavy metal doors," Holiday said. "As soon as we entered, the doors closed.

PRAYER AGAINST ENEMY

Samuel Holiday's group was fortunate to get a ten-day furlough after their training. He returned home, where his father performed a ceremony for him. It was a Prayer against Enemy, which included elements from the Blessing Way and the Enemy Way. "My protection ceremony blessed me with courage and safety before going to war," Holiday said.[4]

Our Navajo teachers stood in front of the room, opened their books, and went through each word, emphasizing and covering every bit of it."[5]

The students worked in groups. Most work was oral, but they also had to understand proper spelling. Holiday felt the Navajo who spoke better English had an advantage. His own English was shaky, but he improved and passed his test on time.

JOHNSTON'S INVOLVEMENT

Philip Johnston, who had originally suggested basing a code on Navajo, wanted to remain involved. He asked to join the Marines in order to work at the school. He was accepted as an administrator for the school. He sometimes acted as a liaison between the Navajo instructors and the Marine Corps commanders. However, he was not personally involved in developing the code.

IN TRAINING

The training course lasted approximately eight weeks. The students also had to learn Morse code, even though they would not be using it for their transmissions. This led to frustrations among both students and teachers. The instructor assigned to teach Morse code, Thomas Randant, recalled rowdy students who did not want to learn. "I believe I lost my temper, health, good disposition and faith in my fellow man over that group of students," he recalled.[6]

Still, he did not fault the students for not wanting to learn the tedious code. "Reading this code is akin to hitting one's self on the head with a hammer," he claimed. "There is no joy in the accomplishment, but it feels so good when you stop." The students resented the enforced learning that was so similar to their school days. During breaks, "They resorted to hand-to-hand physical mayhem to satisfy their need for exercise," Randant recalled.[7]

The new students may have been rowdy during breaks, but they worked hard in the classroom. They learned up to 25 code words a day. The 13-week course covered many areas of training. All codes were to be written entirely in capital letters, to avoid confusion that might come from longhand writing. The code talkers therefore had to practice writing quickly, clearly, and always in capitals. They were graded on spelling and penmanship as well as knowledge of the code words.

They also studied the Navajo alphabet and vocabulary. They learned how to tie, splice, and lay wire. They studied pole climbing, message center operation, voice procedure, and telephone and switchboard operation. They became familiar with several types of radio and wire equipment. The final two weeks included field exercises and the use and repair of equipment.

The students also had to prepare to do their job under extreme conditions. They might be in combat for long hours, under stress, but they could not risk mistakes. Code talker William Kien explained, "Throughout the war against the Japanese in the Pacific, we code talkers had to brush up on our codes at every opportunity. When the fighting got bad, words would fail us for a second."[8] Intensive training

CLAIMING FLUENCY

Recruiter Frank Shannon was a former superintendent of a BIA school system. He believed white people were more intelligent and better at English than the Navajo. He suggested recruiting three white men who had grown up around the Navajo reservation. They claimed they spoke fluent Navajo, and Shannon believed they would make good teachers and interpreters. However, no white man made it through the code talker program. The missionary and trading post families usually only knew enough Navajo to carry on basic conversations.

Marine Private First Class Cecil G. Trosin operates a communication system in the field.

could save lives—their own and the hundreds of soldiers dependent on their ability to interpret codes accurately.

READY FOR WAR

In each class of code talkers, a few stayed behind as instructors. These men eventually rotated out for combat and others took over. The instructors made sure trainees met strict qualifications. Character was as important as intelligence, language skills, and physical abilities. Jimmie King was a member of the second class of code talkers who then became an instructor. He emphasized the importance of keeping the code secret, even under torture. He would not certify a soldier as a code talker unless he was willing to bet his own life on that man. King said, "We knew that a man had good character. You could trust that man. He wouldn't lie to you. He would lay his life down, just like we would, before we would tell what this [the code] was."[9]

Despite the difficulty of the program, only approximately 5 percent of the students failed.[10] Yet even after the Navajo code talkers had proven themselves in school, some officials doubted their ability to do the job. In January 1945, the Fourth and Fifth Marine Divisions embarked for Saipan to load supplies before heading to Iwo Jima. Lieutenant Colonel J. P. Berkeley, Chief Operations Officer of the Signal Corps, Fifth Division, set up a demonstration. He put two Navajo code talkers below deck and two topside. Pairs of white radio operators were set up in similar positions. Each man below deck received a two-and-a-half-paragraph typed report. The lower deck operators sent their message to their counterparts on the upper deck. The Navajos used their code, while the white operators used traditional coding techniques.

IMPROVING THE CODE

Later groups of code talkers expanded on the original code. When the code was first developed, one Navajo word represented each letter. With only one option, a code breaker might be able to see patterns for frequently used letters. The second class of Navajo students added two more words for each vowel. Other common letters also got an additional word. That meant a code talker needing to transmit the letter A had three choices. He could use the Navajo word for ant, apple, or axe. An English word with three As could use each of the three Navajo options in the spelling. A word could also be spelled differently each time it was used in a message. Having several spelling options for every English word made it harder to find patterns. The later code talkers also added more military terms. In the end, the code included 700 words.

Berkeley reported:

> The test took about twenty-five minutes. . . . The Navajos sent their transmission topside with very few errors; the text of the message was not lost. The white operators did very poorly and never completed the entire message. This demonstration convinced a number of senior officers that the Navajos could be accurate and efficient with these types of messages and should be used without hesitation."[11]

Navajo code talker Corporal Lloyd Oliver of Shiprock, New Mexico, operates a radio in the South Pacific.

Code talkers PFC Joe Hosteen Kelwood, Private Floyd Saupitty, and PFC Alex Williams head out for Japanese war fronts on March 31, 1945.

JOINING THE TROOPS

The code talkers had been well trained by the time they shipped out. However, so were the Japanese soldiers, who went through a brutal boot camp. The Imperial Japanese Army instructed soldiers to never retreat and never surrender. "Bear in mind the fact that to be captured means not only that you disgrace yourself, but your parents and family will never be able to hold up their heads again. Always save the last bullet for yourself," their instruction manual said.[1]

Code talkers first served at Guadalcanal. This island in the Solomon chain is 90 miles (145 km) long and 25 miles (40 km) wide. The Japanese had control of it and hoped to use the island as a base to invade Australia and New Zealand. They began building an airfield, which was expected to be operational in August 1942. The Allies wanted that airfield. It would help protect the supply lines between Australia and US forces. Controlling the island could also allow the Allies to drive the Japanese out of the South Pacific, one island at a time.

US Marines landed on the island on August 7, 1942. Initial success turned into a long, drawn-out battle. Both sides lost ships and soldiers. Diseases such as malaria and dysentery made life even more miserable. After weeks of fighting, US troops needed medicine, fresh food, and more weapons. They also needed a more secure means of communication. They had discovered the Japanese were intercepting US radio transmissions.

A supply convoy arrived seven weeks after the initial landing. Along with supplies, on September 18, this convoy brought the first Navajo code talkers, 13 of the men who had developed the code. They were assigned as replacements, without a regular outfit. Neither the code talkers nor the local commanders knew exactly what they were supposed to do. When the code talkers found signal officer Lieutenant Hunt, he decided to try them out right away. William McCabe reported,

> He scattered us to different locations with jeeps that had radios and we began transmitting a routine message. Before we could get through, the whole island was phoning in to ask if the Japanese had broken into our frequency. All the radio operators were trying to jam our message, and Hunt finally had to get on the radio and tell them to stop.[2]

Later, the Navajo operators began transmissions with the tag words "New Mexico" or "Arizona" to let other radio operators know they were part of the US forces.

The following morning, Hunt decided to test the Navajos against a code machine. It usually took four hours for a message to be coded, sent, and deciphered with the machine. McCabe claimed the Navajos could do it in two minutes. Hunt laughed at the idea, but when the code talkers finished in two and a half minutes, he became a believer.

The months on Guadalcanal introduced the Navajo code talkers to combat. They created the first secure network of combat communication, known as the Navajo Net.

CONFUSION AND DANGER

Because the code was kept secret, most commanders did not know much about it until a code-talking unit arrived. That meant the code talkers had to prove themselves every time. Some officers hesitated to give secret messages to these new arrivals, especially since the officers could not understand the words being transmitted. The code talkers were ordered not to explain the code or even give messages to any officer with fewer than three stars. That meant the code talkers often had to refuse orders from soldiers with higher ranks.

Code talkers worked in teams of two. They would help set up the communications system. This could include laying wire to the outposts and setting up the field headquarters radio. Once a station was established, a code

GUADALCANAL

The Japanese finally abandoned Guadalcanal on February 7, 1943. This battle lasted the longest of any fighting in the Pacific. Ten percent of the US force of 60,000 were injured or killed. The Japanese force of 36,000 suffered a two-thirds casualty rate.[3]

Stationed in the South Pacific, PFC Preston Toledo and PFC Frank Toledo sent messages in the Navajo language using a field radio.

talker had to be available at all times. The two men might take turns on duty or they might both work together around the clock.

Code talkers often had to take radios out with combat patrols. They were sometimes sent behind enemy lines as scouts, where they radioed back their reports. The Japanese could intercept these messages. They could not understand the code, but they could identify where it came from. In addition, some of the radios had a hand crank that was loud enough to give away the user's position. The code talkers had to move on immediately after finishing a report or risk facing capture or an enemy attack.

Another complication arose because, to many US soldiers, the Navajo looked Japanese. Several code talkers reported close calls with confused soldiers on their own side who tried to arrest them. Eventually, nearly every code talker

A NAVAJO PRISONER OF WAR

Navajo Joe Kieyoomia joined the army before the code talker program was started. He was stationed in the Philippines, where he was taken prisoner by the Japanese. His name and features persuaded his captors he was of Japanese descent. They accused him of betraying his country and tortured him. Months later, he convinced them he was Navajo. Then the Japanese had Kieyoomia listen to radio broadcasts. He recognized Navajo, but because he did not know the code, he could not understand the message. He was tortured again. Kieyoomia spent 43 months in Japanese prison camps. He was finally freed after the bombing of Nagasaki. He learned about the code talkers years later. "I salute the Code Talkers," he said, "and even if I knew about their code, I wouldn't tell the Japanese."[4]

had a non-Navajo bodyguard who accompanied him everywhere. One of these bodyguards later reported that his unit had been told, "the Code Talkers were a valuable weapon and their safety was first and foremost."[5] However, it was even more important to protect the code itself. Bodyguards had orders to shoot any code talker who was captured by the Japanese. No code talkers were ever captured. In February 1943, the Japanese abandoned Guadalcanal.

THE WAR GOES ON

Navajo code talkers served in every battle in the Pacific from Guadalcanal onward. Many commanders did not understand how the code talkers could be so fast and accurate, but they learned to depend on them.

The code talkers were important to many US military successes, none more so than on Iwo Jima. US forces landed on Iwo Jima on February 19, 1945. Six Navajo Nets operated constantly during the first 48 hours. They sent and received more than 800 messages without a single error.[6]

Samuel Billison remembered the intensity of that time:

> On D-Day the marines went in, but I was kept on the ship to help coordinate naval gunfire. We were supposed to work in six-hour shifts with four hours off in between, but the first two days at Iwo there were no shifts. We were sending message after message for hours on end. . . . I thought that it was rougher duty being on the ship than being on shore. The third day we went in with the 5th Division on the third wave. Once we landed, I found out what rough really was.[7]

The dangerous attack on Iwo Jima left many US troops dead.

RAISING THE FLAG

A famous photo shows six Marines raising a flag on the summit of Mount Suribachi. This was not the first flag raised, but rather a larger one raised later that morning as a replacement. The photo became a symbol of victory and patriotism. President Franklin D. Roosevelt called the flag raisers heroes. The three who survived Iwo Jima were sent on a national publicity tour to promote war bonds. One of these men was Ira Hayes, who was a member of a Native American group known as the Pima. Hayes did not like the publicity and had trouble adjusting to civilian life after the war. He developed a drinking problem, which killed him at age 32. He is buried at Arlington National Cemetery in Virginia. A bronze statue replicating the photo stands in Arlington Cemetery as a monument to all Marines who gave their lives to defend their country.

The day after the landing, Marines secured the southern end of the island. They then pushed forward with the mission of securing Mount Suribachi. When they reached the top, they hoisted the American flag. Code talkers sent the message throughout the Pacific that the flag had been raised.

That symbolic victory was not the end of the battle, however. It lasted for 36 days. Merril Sandoval recalled the Japanese trying to distract the code talkers by shouting, singing, or banging on pots. He explained,

> Our messages went through because we knew each other's voices and the code so well that we could do it without any repeat or mistakes. On Iwo we were told that if we had a message, get it through the first time accurately, and then get off the radio. The familiarity with each other and the confidence we had in the code made it possible for us to do just that."[8]

Some 6,800 US troops, including three code talkers, died on Iwo Jima.[9] The battle also marked an important turning point in the war. The United States gained a valuable airfield. B-29 bombers made approximately 24,000 emergency landings during the remaining months of the war.

This poster by artist Cecil Calvert Beall depicts American soldiers raising the flag on Iwo Jima.

This group of Meskwaki men from Tama, Iowa, joined the US Army. They were one of the 16 Native American tribes with members working as code talkers during the war.

OTHER TRIBES

The Navajo were by far the largest group of code talkers used during World War II. However, soldiers from many tribes served, using their native languages to send secure messages. While the Marines developed the Navajo code, other branches of the military looked to other Native Americans for assistance. Code talkers were recruited from many tribes. Altogether, members of at least 16 tribes served as code talkers for the army, the navy, and Marines. Some were drafted. Others enlisted voluntarily, and some, as young as 15 years old, lied about their age in order to join.

Other soldiers got recruited as code talkers after they had enlisted as regular soldiers. In January 1941, 27 men from the tiny Meskwaki tribe had enlisted in the Iowa National Guard. Eight of them received special training in the use of the walkie-talkie radio and became code talkers. In November 1942, the Meskwaki code talkers were deployed in Algiers, North Africa, with infantry troops, fighting against the Germans. Later the Meskwaki code talkers joined the campaign in Italy. The eight code talkers worked 24-hour shifts, sending messages between the eight companies in the division.

Clarence Wolf Guts of the Oglala Lakota enlisted in the US Army in 1942 at age 18. He went to basic training, where a general asked if he spoke Sioux. Wolf Guts explained that Sioux has different dialects and he spoke Lakota. He went on to help develop a phonetic alphabet based on Lakota. This was later used to develop a code. Wolf Guts served as a code talker in the Pacific, transmitting messages from a general to his chief of staff in the field.

Regardless of how they entered the military, code talkers worked and fought together in teams. In some cases, they sent messages using their everyday language. For a "Type Two Code," secrecy was not as important. This might be a message such as "Send more ammunition to the front." This could be sent over the radio in the code talker's native language, or even in English.

NATIVE WARRIORS

Many Native Americans fought in World War II without becoming code talkers. Approximately 44,000 men and women from different tribes served. This was more than 12 percent of the total Native American population of 350,000.[1] This is about the same percentage as soldiers from the general population at the time, but far greater than the 0.5 percent of Americans who serve today.[2]

A "Type One Code" required additional security. Along with the Navajo, members of tribes such as the Comanches, Hopis, and Meskwakis developed special codes. These codes used words in the native language to represent letters

MILITARY HONORS

Native Americans served in every branch of the military, performing a variety of duties. Many received military honors, with at least 30 receiving the Distinguished Flying Cross. This is the highest aviation honor given for heroism and extraordinary achievement while participating in aerial flight. Sergeant Shuman Shaw, a Paiute who served as a tail-gunner, shot down several of the enemy after he was wounded on a mission. Lieutenant William R. Fredenberg, a Menominee, "demonstrated superior skill in the execution of a dive-bombing attack upon a heavily defended marshalling yard wherein he personally destroyed three locomotives." His citation adds that he "thereafter in the face of heavy and accurate enemy fire remained in the target area strafing installations until his ammunition was exhausted."[3] Some awards were given posthumously to soldiers who died during the war.

of the English alphabet. When military terms could not easily be translated, they came up with words to fit.

In the field, code talkers received messages in English. They translated these into their native language without writing them down. Then they transmitted the messages to another code talker. At the receiving end, the code talker translated the message back to English and wrote it down.

DANGEROUS TIMES

It might seem that being a code talker, operating a radio, would be safer than being one of the fighters. However, this was not always the case. In North Africa, the Meskwaki code talkers acted as scouts as the troops moved toward Tunisia. Scouts had to take the lead and move quickly across difficult terrain with heavy equipment, establishing posts for observation and communication. "It was the worst place this side of hell," Frank Sanache said.[4] Three of the code talkers were captured by the enemy. As prisoners of war, they were starved, beaten, and tortured.

Sanache was captured by the Germans and became a prisoner of war. He was held at a camp in Poland for 29 months, until the end of the war. He had to work unloading railcars, despite never having enough to eat. "A cup of hot water in the morning for coffee," he explained in an interview. "A little bowl of soup at noon, then two potatoes at night. That's what you live on. That's what I lived on for three years."[5] Another Meskwaki code talker, Dewey Youngbear, made multiple escape attempts but was recaptured each time.

For many soldiers, religious beliefs helped them get through the hardest times. Hopi Franklin Shupla said, "We prayed to the sun, stars, whatever. It's our way of keeping in contact with somebody. Our superior or whatever you might call him. That's how we do it."[6]

PRISONERS OF WAR

Conditions were often horrific in prisoner of war camps. Thousands of soldiers died from starvation, mistreatment, or disease. Hundreds of Native Americans were captured and spent time as prisoners of war. Some spent several years in captivity. In some cases, families had no idea whether their sons were dead or alive. Chippewa Omar Schoenborn was believed dead after the prison ship carrying him to Japan was sunk. However, he swam ashore and hid from the Japanese until the American forces arrived.

COMANCHE RETURN

The US Army hoped to replicate the successful code talking accomplished at the end of World War I. The army sent special recruiters to find Comanches in Oklahoma. Seventeen Comanche men enlisted in the US Army and received

Comanche code talkers of the US Army's Fourth Signal Company took time from training to pose for a photo at Fort Gordon, near Augusta, Georgia.

training as radio operators. They developed a secret code no one else would be able to understand, not even other Comanches. The code included a dictionary of 100 words. Some military terms did not exist in Comanche, so they had to be replaced with other words.

Charles Chibitty explained, "Well, when they first got us in there for Code Talkers, we had to work that out among our own selves so, we didn't have a word for tank." Someone pointed out that a tank is like a turtle. "It has a hard shell and it moves and so we called it a wakaree´e, a turtle."[7]

Fourteen Comanche code talkers fought in Europe, 13 of them landing at Normandy on D-Day on June 6, 1944. However, when their division landed, they were five miles (8 km) off their target. The first message sent included, "Tsaaku nunnuwee. Atahtu nunnuwee." In translation, it said, "We made a good landing. We landed in the wrong place."[8]

The division managed to join the battle, though, facing some of the fiercest fighting of the war. Chibitty later said in an interview, "Utah Beach in Normandy was something else. Everybody asked me if I would go through it again, and I said, no, but I could train the younger ones how we used our language and let them go ahead and do it because it was hell."[9] While some Comanche code talkers were wounded, all survived the war. Their code was never broken.

CHARLES CHIBITTY

1921–2005

Charles Chibitty was one of the 17 Comanche soldiers trained as code talkers. Born in Oklahoma in 1921, he attended a Native American school where he was punished for speaking his native language.

Chibitty joined the US Army in 1940. He trained in Georgia with 16 other Comanche soldiers. Chibitty participated in several major battles, including D-Day in Normandy. He attained the rank of corporal and earned five campaign battle stars. His tribe awarded him a cavalry officer's saber, the Comanche equivalent of a Medal of Honor.

After the war, Chibitty became a respected leader of his people. He worked as a glazier, installing glass windows in buildings. He taught the Comanche language, believing it important to preserve his culture. He was a champion in powwow dance contests and also participated in gourd dances, special dances to honor veterans.

Chibitty was honored at the Pentagon and received several special awards. Chibitty, the last of the Comanche code talkers, died in 2005.

PFC George H. Kirk and PFC John V. Goodluck enlisted in the US Marine Corps in 1943 and served in Guam.

END OF THE WAR

The Navajo Net remained an important asset to US troops until
Japan finally surrendered on August 14, 1945. The Japanese had
been able to break codes used by the US Army and US Army Air
Corps. They were never able to break the Navajo code used by the
Marines. Eleven Navajo code talkers are known to have been killed
in action, including one of the original 29, Harry Tsosie. Many
others suffered close calls.

Though few people knew about their real mission, the Navajo
were recognized as excellent soldiers. They took on many tasks
besides operating radios. They benefited from the physical fitness
and comfort in rough terrain they had acquired during their days
on the reservation. Many commanding officers praised them,
including one who said, "As general duty Marines, the Navajos are
without peers."[1]

REPORTING THE BOMBINGS

Some of the last messages sent in the Navajo code reported on the atomic bombs that were dropped on Hiroshima and Nagasaki. Because this was the first time the bombs were used in warfare, scientists wanted to know exactly what happened. Army and navy personnel prepared reports to be sent back to scientists in the United States. For security, these were transmitted in the Navajo code.

Code talkers from other tribes also contributed to US success during the war. Many code talkers received medals such as Silver Stars and Purple Hearts. These awards were given for specific acts of heroism or for injuries sustained during battle. However, the military did not offer any specific recognition for code talking.

The Navajo code talkers were instructed to stay silent on their specific duties. Military officials wanted to keep the code secret in case it was needed again. Nez explained,

When we got out, discharged, they told us this thing that you guys did is going to be a secret. When you get home you don't talk about what you did; don't tell your people, your parents, family, don't tell them what your job was. . . . Just tell them you were in the service, defend your country and stuff like that. But, the code, never, never, don't mention; don't talk about it.[2]

Code talkers from other tribes were not necessarily instructed to remain silent. However, they seldom shared the information outside their own communities and did not receive official recognition.

BACK TO CIVILIAN LIFE

Soldiers often struggle to adjust to civilian life after a war. This can be especially difficult when the soldiers are not allowed to talk about their experiences. Dan Akee had nightmares for more than a year. "Every time I shut my eyes I would see or hear the enemy coming at me, and I'd find myself screaming."[3] He went deaf, but doctors could find no reason.

Dan Akee's father arranged a gourd dance for him. "The first night I heard a drum and my ear popped and I could hear again! . . . After the Gourd Dance, I gained back my weight, and the nightmares slowly faded."[4]

Native American cultures recognize how participating in war upsets the balance of life. Special ceremonies are designed to bring back balance. Among traditional Navajos, a family may sponsor a ceremony when a soldier returns from war. A spiritual leader consults with the soldier and decides which ceremony will help. For soldiers who were in combat, wounded, or captured, this might be the Enemy Way, also called the squaw dance. Family members and other people often join in the prayers, songs, and other activities. These ceremonies helped some code talkers find a sense of balance, or *Hozho* in Navajo.

Navajo code talker John Brown Jr. said that after the war,

> I had nightmares thinking about the blood. The Japanese and the smell of the dead. Rotting Japanese and they probably got into my mind. And they had a Squaw Dance for me in Crystal. And I imagine they killed that evil spirit that was in my mind. . . . It takes a long time to talk about it. It usually takes a medicine man to explain everything properly. But it works.[5]

Even those who left behind traditional beliefs sometimes found comfort in them. Carl Gorman had been raised Christian, but when a medicine man offered to do a one-night ceremony for free, Gorman agreed. "I participated in the sing and felt a great weight leave my mind and body. I felt very rested afterwards. I realized then that I needed to make peace with what I had experienced during the war."[6]

Many Native Americans are also Christian and draw on the services and prayers of Christian churches for healing. The Native American Church combines Christianity with traditional Native American ceremonies. It helped many Comanche and others recover from the effects of war.

A HARD LIFE

After World War II, jobs were in short supply. So were basic items such as food and gasoline. Native American communities had often struggled with poverty and unemployment. After the war, it was even more difficult to find work or job training. In addition, racism continued. Native American veterans still could not vote in some states. Samuel Holiday remembered being turned away from hotels and restaurants. "The people did not care about veterans, my going to war meant nothing to them; it seemed just like having a good horse, working it hard until the job was finished, then chasing it away."[7]

Some former code talkers stayed in the military. Others went back to work as farmers or ranchers. Many also moved to American cities to find jobs. Some veterans used the G.I. Bill, which helped them go to college or get vocational training.

Despite the difficulties, many code talkers tried to help protect their native culture. They participated in tribal governments and helped preserve their language and way of life. Some became teachers, artists, or other professionals. Many recognized the importance of education, along with the importance of their ancient beliefs and practices. They

NO VOTE

Largely due to their contributions during World War I, Native Americans who had not yet obtained US citizenship received it under the Indian Citizenship Act of 1924. However, they still could not vote in some states. New Mexico and Arizona granted Native Americans the right to vote in 1948. Utah waited until 1957.

helped blend modern knowledge and traditional teachings for the following generations. "It was a very interesting ride that we had, serving as Navajo Code Talkers," Roy Hawthorne said. "It opened our eyes to the fact that we were achievers. . . . By my life and my actions and teachings, I see my grandchildren, my great grandchildren knowing what this country stands for."[8]

This monument stands at Window Rock, Arizona, in honor of the contributions made by all the Navajo code talkers during World War II.

TELLING THE STORY

The code talker program was finally declassified in 1968. People around the world began recognizing the important contributions of the code talkers. The first public recognition came in 1969. The Fourth Marine Division held an

Several Native American tribes received Congressional Gold Medals on November 20, 2013. The awards recognize code talkers who served in both world wars.

CARL GORMAN

1908–1998

As a child, Carl Gorman ran away from a mission school. He later attended the Albuquerque Indian School. He joined the US Marine Corps in 1942 and was one of the original 29 Navajo code talkers. He served in four important Pacific battles, including Guadalcanal. He continued to fight even after getting malaria, but in 1944, he was hospitalized for malaria and shell shock. His recovery took many months.

After the war, Gorman studied at the Otis Art Institute in California. He went on to draw technical illustrations for an aircraft company and to become a successful artist. He painted scenes of his homeland and culture. He was also involved in the Navajo Club in Los Angeles, which organized shipments of food and clothing to help people on the Navajo reservation.

Gorman became a college professor at the University of California at Davis. Later he worked for the Navajo government and the Navajo Community College. Gorman died in 1998, before the Navajos received their Congressional Medals of Honor, but he received many other awards in his lifetime.

"There are a thousand paths you can take in life," he said. "But there is only one right one. . . . when you're on the right path, you'll know it."[9]

annual reunion and always gave a special honor to a member. Committee member Lee Cannon suggested they recognize the code talkers. Twenty code talkers attended, including 15 who had served in the Fourth Division. One code talker represented each of the other five divisions.

In 1971, a two-day code talker reunion was held at Window Rock, Arizona. Interviewers recorded the code talkers telling their stories. These interviews provided more information on the role of code talkers in the war. The 69 code talkers present organized the Code Talkers Association. John Benally, one of the original 29 Navajo code talkers, became the chairman. The association's goal was to educate people about the role the code talkers played during the war. They began marching in the Veterans Day parades, visiting schools, and making national appearances.

Later in 1971, President Richard Nixon presented the Navajo code talkers with a certificate of appreciation. Other recognitions slowly followed. August 14, 1982, was officially designated as National Navajo Code Talkers Day. President Ronald Reagan issued the proclamation and called upon both officials and citizens to join in the tribute.

News of the National Navajo Code Talkers Day reached Japan. The *Fuji Evening* newspaper reported on the event and explained how the code talkers had altered the course of the war: "Without the activities of the Navajo tribe, the history of the Pacific War might have turned out completely different."[10]

US allies also recognized the importance of the code talkers. The Comanche code talkers, who had fought in Europe, received a high honor from the French government in 1989. A representative of the Northern Mariana Islands held a banquet in Window Rock in 1994. He personally thanked the code talkers for their part in helping end Japanese control of the Pacific.

The Navajo code talkers received special US Congressional Medals in 2001. The original 29 were awarded gold medals, and those who joined the program later received silver medals. On the back of the medals, a message in Navajo states, "With the Navajo language they defeated the enemy."[11]

President George W. Bush presented the medals at the White House. He said, "Gentlemen, your service inspires the respect and admiration of all Americans, and our gratitude is expressed for all time, in the medals it is now my honor to present."[12] Many code talkers passed away before the medals were awarded. Other family members accepted the medals on their behalf. Some state, local, and tribal governments, along with a variety of other organizations, have also offered special recognition to the code talkers.

Of the approximately 3,600 Navajos who served in the US military during World War II, approximately 420 were code talkers.[13] Dozens of other code talkers came from different tribes. Only a few are still alive. Chester Nez summed up their contribution. "My fellow code talkers and I have become part of a new oral and written tradition, a Navajo victory, with our culture contributing to our country's defeat of a wily foe. . . . Our story is not one of sorrow . . . but one of triumph."[14]

Honored Navajo Code Talkers take part in the Veteran's Day parade along New York's Fifth Avenue on November 11, 2012.

TIMELINE

1918
Choctaw code talkers help US forces take a German stronghold in France.

1924
All Native Americans born in the United States receive US citizenship.

September 1939
Germany invades Poland, igniting World War II in Europe.

December 7, 1941
Japan attacks the US naval base at Pearl Harbor. Within days, America is at war with Japan, Germany, and Italy.

September 18, 1942
The first Navajo code talkers join combat forces at Guadalcanal.

November 1942
Meskwaki code talkers in the Thirty-Fourth Infantry advance on the beaches of Algeria, North Africa.

June 6, 1944
Comanche code talkers are with Allied troops when they land in France on D-Day.

February 19, 1945
The United States invades Iwo Jima. Navajo Nets operate for 48 hours straight.

June 4–7, 1942

The United States stages a successful ambush at Midway Island.

June 27, 1942

The first group of Navajo code talkers graduates from boot camp.

August 7, 1942

US Marines land at Guadalcanal.

September 1942

The first Navajo code talkers finish their training, having developed a working code.

1968

The Navajo code talker program is declassified.

1971

The Code Talkers Association is founded at a code talker reunion.

August 14, 1982

The first official Navajo National Code Talkers Day is declared. This later becomes an annual event on August 14.

2001

The Navajo code talkers receive special US Congressional Medals.

ESSENTIAL FACTS

KEY PLAYERS

- Philip Johnston, the son of white missionaries, grows up on a Navajo Reservation and can speak the language fluently. After the attack on Pearl Harbor in December 1941, Johnston suggests to the US Marines they use the Navajo language to develop a code for use during World War II.

- John Benally is one of the original 29 Navajos recruited for the code talker program in May 1942 and is promoted to corporal. At this new rank, his job is to teach a new round of recruits the Navajo code.

- Johnny Manuelito, like Benally, is one of the original Navajo code talkers who helps devise the code. He is also promoted to corporal and hired to teach the second round of recruits the Navajo code.

THE LANGUAGES OF WAR

The following languages are used during World War II to send secret military messages. Each tribe provides at least two code talkers. If the total number is known, it is listed after the tribe.

- Navajo (about 420) serve in the Pacific in battles against the Japanese

- Sac and Fox/Meskwaki (19) serve in North Africa against the Germans

- Chippewa/Oneida (17)

- Comanche (17) serve in Europe against the Germans

- Hopi (11) serve in the Pacific against the Japanese

- Assiniboine

- Cherokee

- Choctaw

- Kiowa

- Menominee

- Muscogee/Creek and Seminole

- Pawnee

- Sioux—Lakota and Dakota dialects

IMPACT ON THE WAR

The code talkers provide a major advantage to the United States in World War II. They send thousands of messages, with great accuracy, in codes that are never broken. Their actions save lives and help win battles.

IMPACT ON SOCIETY

By developing the Navajo Net, the US military gains a distinct advantage over Japan, Germany, and Italy during World War II. This advantage is enough to win the war, forever altering history.

QUOTE

"My fellow code talkers and I have become part of a new oral and written tradition, a Navajo victory, with our culture contributing to our country's defeat of a wily foe. . . . Our story is not one of sorrow . . . but one of triumph."

—Chester Nez, Navajo Code Talker

GLOSSARY

ARMADA

A fleet of warships.

ARTILLERY

Large guns or missile launchers, as distinguished from small arms; also, the troops or branch of the military that uses these weapons.

BLOCKADE

To isolate or close off a place to prevent people or goods from entering or leaving.

CASUALTY

A person who is injured, missing, or killed during a military campaign.

CIPHER

A code or disguised way of writing.

D-DAY

The day on which an attack or military operation is to begin.

DECLASSIFIED

To declare information no longer secret.

FURLOUGH

A leave of absence.

G.I. BILL
A law passed in 1944 to provide benefits for people who had served in the armed forces in World War II.

PHONETIC
A written element that represents a sound.

POSTHUMOUS
Happening after someone's death.

RESERVATION
Land set aside for a Native American tribe, often smaller than their traditional lands.

SHELL SHOCK
Feelings of distress, panic, or helplessness that can last after an exposure to trauma, today called post-traumatic stress.

ADDITIONAL RESOURCES

SELECTED BIBLIOGRAPHY

Holiday, Samuel, and Robert S. McPherson. *Under the Eagle: Samuel Holiday, Navajo Code Talker*. Norman, OK: U of Oklahoma P, 2013. Print.

Mack, Stephen. *It Had to Be Done: The Navajo Code Talkers Remember World War II*. Tucson, AZ: Whispering Dove Design, 2008. Print.

McClain, S. *Navajo Weapon*. Boulder, CO: Books Beyond Borders, 1994. Print.

Nez, Chester, with Judith Schiess Avila. *Code Talker*. New York: Berkley Caliber, 2011. Print.

FURTHER READINGS

Bearce, Stephanie. *Top Secret Files World War II: Spies, Secret Missions, and Hidden Facts from World War II*. Waco, TX: Prufrock, 2014. Print.

Denetdale, Jennifer. *The Navajo*. New York: Chelsea, 2011. Print.

Durrett, Deanne. *Unsung Heroes of World War II: The Story of the Navajo Code Talkers*. Lincoln: U of Nebraska P, 2009. Print.

WEBSITES

To learn more about Essential Library of World War II, visit **booklinks.abdopublishing.com**. These links are routinely monitored and updated to provide the most current information available.

PLACES TO VISIT

The National Cryptologic Museum
8290 Colony Seven Road
Annapolis Junction, MD 20701
301-688-5849
https://www.nsa.gov/about/cryptologic_heritage/museum
Visitors can learn about the history of American code making and code breaking through many exhibits, including one on the Native American code talkers.

National Museum of the American Indian
Fourth Street & Independence Avenue SW
Washington, DC 20560
202-633-5285
http://www.nmai.si.edu/visit/washington
The NMAI holds one of the world's largest collections of Native American artifacts, including objects and photographs. Special events and daily hands-on activities are directed at families.

National Museum of the US Air Force
1100 Spaatz Street
Wright-Patterson AFB OH 45433
937-255-3286
http://www.nationalmuseum.af.mil
A World War II Gallery houses a collection of World War II aircraft, including the B-29 Bockscar, which dropped the atomic bomb on Nagasaki, Japan.

SOURCE NOTES

CHAPTER 1. IN THE HEAT OF BATTLE

1. "Iwo Jima." *Encyclopedia Britannica*. Encyclopedia Britannica, 12 May 2014. Web. 9 Mar. 2015.

2. Sally McClain. *Navajo Weapon*. Boulder, CO: Books Beyond Borders, 1994. Print. 161.

3. Ibid. 166.

4. Deanne Durrett. *Unsung Heroes of World War II: The Story of the Navajo Code Talkers*. Lincoln: U of Nebraska P, 2009. Print. 86.

5. Sally McClain. *Navajo Weapon*. Boulder, CO: Books Beyond Borders, 1994. Print. 168.

CHAPTER 2. SECRETS OF WAR

1. Sally McClain. *Navajo Weapon*. Boulder, CO: Books Beyond Borders, 1994. Print. 21–22.

2. Ibid. 21.

3. "Pearl Harbor." *History.com*. A+E Television, 2015. Web. 9 Mar. 2015.

CHAPTER 3. THE PEOPLE

1. John Rehling. "Native American Languages." *The Center for Research on Concepts and Cognition*. Indiana University, n.d. Web. 4 Nov 2014.

2. "Boarding Schools." *NMAI*. National Museum of the American Indian, n.d. Web. 9 Mar. 2015.

3. Chester Nez with Judith Schiess Avila. *Code Talker*. New York: Berkley Caliber, 2011. Print. 104.

4. Sally McClain. *Navajo Weapon*. Boulder, CO: Books Beyond Borders, 1994. Print. 25–28.

5. "Living the Culture." *NMAI*. National Museum of the American Indian, n.d. Web. 9 Mar. 2015.

6. Nancy C. Maryboy and David Begay. "Utah's Native Americans: Chapter 7 – the Navajos of Utah." *Utah History to Go*. State of Utah, 2014. Web. 9 Mar. 2015.

7. Samuel Holiday and Robert S. McPherson. *Under the Eagle: Samuel Holiday, Navajo Code Talker*. Norman: U of Oklahoma P, 2013. Print. 84.

8. "Recognition." *NMAI*. National Museum of the American Indian, n.d. Web. 9 Mar. 2015.

9. Deanne Durrett. *Unsung Heroes of World War II: The Story of the Navajo Code Talkers*. Lincoln: U of Nebraska P, 2009. Print. 4–6.

10. Ibid.

CHAPTER 4. RECRUITMENT AND TRAINING

1. Sally McClain. *Navajo Weapon*. Boulder, CO: Books Beyond Borders, 1994. Print. 38.

2. Deanne Durrett. *Unsung Heroes of World War II: The Story of the Navajo Code Talkers*. Lincoln: U of Nebraska P, 2009. Print. 30.

3. "Boarding Schools." *NMAI*. National Museum of the American Indian, n.d. Web. 9 Mar. 2015.

4. Sally McClain. *Navajo Weapon*. Boulder, CO: Books Beyond Borders, 1994. Print. 41.

5. Chester Nez with Judith Schiess Avila. *Code Talker*. New York: Berkley Caliber, 2011. Print. 94–99.

6. Deanne Durrett. *Unsung Heroes of World War II: The Story of the Navajo Code Talkers*. Lincoln: U of Nebraska P, 2009. Print. 25–26.

7. Sally McClain. *Navajo Weapon*. Boulder, CO: Books Beyond Borders, 1994. Print. 41–42.

8. Deanne Durrett. *Unsung Heroes of World War II: The Story of the Navajo Code Talkers*. Lincoln: U of Nebraska P, 2009. Print. 29.

9. Sally McClain. *Navajo Weapon*. Boulder, CO: Books Beyond Borders, 1994. Print. 41.

10. Ibid. 45–46.

11. Chester Nez with Judith Schiess Avila. *Code Talker*. New York: Berkley Caliber, 2011. Print. 249–252.

CHAPTER 5. CREATING THE CODE

1. Deanne Durrett. *Unsung Heroes of World War II: The Story of the Navajo Code Talkers*. Lincoln: U of Nebraska P, 2009. Print. 54.

2. Chester Nez with Judith Schiess Avila. *Code Talker*. New York: Berkley Caliber, 2011. Print. 102–3.

3. Ibid. 106.

4. Sally McClain. *Navajo Weapon*. Boulder, CO: Books Beyond Borders, 1994. Print. 54.

5. Deanne Durrett. *Unsung Heroes of World War II: The Story of the Navajo Code Talkers*. Lincoln: U of Nebraska P, 2009. Print. 44.

6. Sally McClain. *Navajo Weapon*. Boulder, CO: Books Beyond Borders, 1994. Print. 56.

7. Chester Nez with Judith Schiess Avila. *Code Talker*. New York: Berkley Caliber, 2011. Print. 108.

8. Sally McClain. *Navajo Weapon*. Boulder, CO: Books Beyond Borders, 1994. Print. 58.

CHAPTER 6. RECRUITING MORE CODE TALKERS

1. "Living the Culture." *NMAI*. National Museum of the American Indian, n.d. Web. 7 Nov. 2014.

2. Sally McClain. *Navajo Weapon*. Boulder, CO: Books Beyond Borders, 1994. Print. 77.

3. Samuel Holiday and Robert S. McPherson. *Under the Eagle: Samuel Holiday, Navajo Code Talker*. Norman: U of Oklahoma P, 2013. Print. 82.

4. Ibid. 83–85.

5. Ibid. 83–87.

6. Sally McClain. *Navajo Weapon*. Boulder, CO: Books Beyond Borders, 1994. Print. 79–80.

7. Ibid. 80.

8. Ibid. 79–80.

9. Deanne Durrett. *Unsung Heroes of World War II: The Story of the Navajo Code Talkers*. Lincoln: U of Nebraska P, 2009. Print. 56.

10. Ibid. 57.

11. Sally McClain. *Navajo Weapon*. Boulder, CO: Books Beyond Borders, 1994. Print. 163.

SOURCE NOTES
CONTINUED

CHAPTER 7. JOINING THE TROOPS

1. Sally McClain. *Navajo Weapon*. Boulder, CO: Books Beyond Borders, 1994. Print. 63.

2. Ibid. 67.

3. Deanne Durrett. *Unsung Heroes of World War II: The Story of the Navajo Code Talkers*. Lincoln: U of Nebraska P, 2009. Print. 62.

4. Tim Korte. "How Effective Was Navajo Code?" *News From Indian Country*. Aug. 1997. Web. *yvwiiusdinvnohii. net*. 9 Mar. 2015.

5. Deanne Durrett. *Unsung Heroes of World War II: The Story of the Navajo Code Talkers*. Lincoln: U of Nebraska P, 2009. Print. 77.

6. Ibid. 86.

7. Sally McClain. *Navajo Weapon*. Boulder, CO: Books Beyond Borders, 1994. Print. 168–169.

8. Ibid. 175.

9. Deanne Durrett. *Unsung Heroes of World War II: The Story of the Navajo Code Talkers*. Lincoln: U of Nebraska P, 2009. Print. 92.

CHAPTER 8. OTHER TRIBES

1. "Code Talking: Intelligence and Bravery." *NMAI*. National Museum of the American Indian, n.d. Web. 9 Mar. 2015.

2. Karl W. Eikenberry and David M. Kennedy. "Americans and Their Military, Drifting Apart." *New York Times*. New York Times, 26 May 2013. Web. 9 Mar. 2015.

3. "Indians in the War 1945." *Naval History and Heritage Command*. US Navy, n.d. Web. 9 Mar. 2015.

4. "Last Meskwaki Code Talker Remembers." *USA Today*. USA Today, 4 July 2002. Web. 9 Mar. 2015.

5. "Code Talking." *NMAI*. National Museum of the American Indian, n.d. Web. 9 Mar. 2015.

6. Ibid.

7. "Code Talking: Intelligence and Bravery." *NMAI*. National Museum of the American Indian, n.d. Web. 9 Mar. 2015.

8. "Comanche Code Talkers." *Comanche National Museum and Cultural Center*. Comanche National Museum and Cultural Center, n.d. Web. 9 Mar. 2015.

9. "Code Talking: Intelligence and Bravery." *NMAI*. National Museum of the American Indian, n.d. Web. 9 Mar. 2015.

CHAPTER 9. END OF THE WAR

1. Deanne Durrett. *Unsung Heroes of World War II: The Story of the Navajo Code Talkers*. Lincoln: U of Nebraska P, 2009. Print. 65.

2. "Recognition." *NMAI*. National Museum of the American Indian, n.d. Web. 9 Mar. 2015.

3. Sally McClain. *Navajo Weapon*. Boulder, CO: Books Beyond Borders, 1994. Print. 227.

4. Ibid.

5. "Coming Home." *NMAI*. National Museum of the American Indian, n.d. Web. 9 Mar. 2015.

6. Ibid.

7. Samuel Holiday and Robert S. McPherson. *Under the Eagle: Samuel Holiday, Navajo Code Talker*. Norman: U of Oklahoma P, 2013. Print. 184.

8. Mark Olalde. "Arizona Code Talkers Get Their Own Day." *AZCentral*. Gannett, 17 July 2014. Web. 9 Mar. 2015.

9. "Survival." *NMAI*. National Museum of the American Indian, n.d. Web. 9 Mar. 2015.

10. Sally McClain. *Navajo Weapon*. Boulder, CO: Books Beyond Borders, 1994. Print. 237.

11. "Recognition." *NMAI*. National Museum of the American Indian, n.d. Web. 9 Mar. 2015.

12. Ibid.

13. Deanne Durrett. *Unsung Heroes of World War II: The Story of the Navajo Code Talkers*. Lincoln: U of Nebraska P, 2009. Print. 98.

14. Chester Nez with Judith Schiess Avila. *Code Talker*. New York: Berkley Caliber, 2011. Print. 265–266.

INDEX

ABOUT THE AUTHOR

Chris Eboch, a.k.a. M. M. Eboch, writes about science, history, and culture for all ages. Her recent nonfiction titles include *Chaco Canyon, Living with Dyslexia,* and *The Green Movement.* Her novels for young people include *The Genie's Gift,* a Middle Eastern fantasy; *The Eyes of Pharaoh,* a mystery in ancient Egypt; *The Well of Sacrifice,* a Mayan adventure; and the Haunted series, which starts with *The Ghost on the Stairs.* Learn more at www.chriseboch.com.

ABOUT THE CONSULTANT

Thomas A. Britten is a history professor at the University of Texas at Brownsville. He has written four books about various aspects of Native American history including *American Indians in World War One* (University of New Mexico Press, 1997) and appeared on the PBS documentary *Way of the Warrior,* which examined the historic role of Native Americans in the US military.